ENGLISH
SILVER
HALL-MARKS

edited by

Judith Banister

with Lists of
English, Scottish and Irish
Hall-marks and Makers Marks

LONDON
W. FOULSHAM & Co. Ltd.
NEW YORK   TORONTO   CAPE TOWN   SYDNEY

W. FOULSHAM & CO. LTD.,

Yeovil Road, Slough, Berks., England.

ISBN 0-572-00674-8

Printed in Hong Kong

CONTENTS

ACKNOWLEDGEMENTS

The Publishers extend their thanks to the Masters of the Assay Offices of Dublin, Sheffield and Birmingham for the advice, guidance and material for reproduction which they were kind enough to supply.

In particular sincere thanks are extended to the Goldsmiths Company for the continuance support and assistance which they gave and for the right to reproduce the majority of Makers' marks from their records.

Also acknowledged is the material reprinted from Goldsmiths & Their Marks by Sir Charles Jackson, Dover Publications, New York through whom permissions were obtained.

PREFACE

The intention underlying the publication of this Pocket Identification Guide has been to provide, for Collectors and Dealers alike, a portable reference source to the Assay Office Marks *and* more important Makers' Marks found on British Silver.

In the tables containing the Assay Office Marks, it will be seen that each cycle has been contained in one box and that to the outside edge of each box an additional panel has been added. This layout was chosen to allow for the inclusion in the panels of an enlarged Assay Office Symbol and Date Letter which we hope will provide for quicker visual location when "flipping through" the pages. This will be of value not only to those who do know something of silver marking but also to those new collectors who know nothing of the devices adopted by the various Assay Offices. It is assumed that these Collectors will carefully read the Introduction to silver marking but for them we would explain that having located the *style* of town mark and date letter in the outside panel all of the remaining marks on the piece in question must be checked against those reproduced in the box. This should confirm that the right period has been located and provide a date of Assay against the relevant date letter.

During the earliest working periods of some of the Assay Offices there is little consistency in the design of marks applied to silver. They change so frequently in the cycle boxes that it has been impossible to include anything very worthwhile in the exterior panels. For consistency, however, we have included the design that seems to be most representative of those in the boxes and hope that they will be of some value.

Finally, attention is drawn to the details of monarchs in each panel. These are included to show which of the sovereigns were reigning during each cycle. Where only one name is given, it can be taken that throughout that period there was no accession to the throne. Where there is a change of rule during the cycle, both monarchs and the date of accession are given.

The Makers' Marks found in the third section of the book are in the main of those whose work was done in London; though obviously we have included the most important makers from Birmingham, Dublin, Edinburgh and Sheffield. We have confined our coverage of them to the period 1697 to 1900 which we felt represented the period from which most antique silver is currently available. Obviously to include every silver maker of that period is out of the question in a book of this length and we therefore compiled a list of renowned or prolific silver makers and illustrated those of their marks which would ensure the identification of all of their work. Our reference source has been the Official records held by the Goldsmiths' Company in London whose permission and kind assistance we had in being allowed to photograph the marks entered by the London makers in the record books. For this reason we can reasonably claim that the section on makers' marks is one of the most accurate records available.

The only qualifying factor we would wish to place on the above statement is that though every mark represents an accurate impression of that entered in the record books, they are not necessarily proportionally accurate one to another. We have had to enlarge each mark for ease of identification but because of the great variety in their sizes and the standard width of our page, have been unable to achieve a standard degree of magnification.

Introduction

SILVER HALL-MARKS

Hall-marks are the authenticating marks struck on all modern and most old English, Scottish and Irish silver and gold. They are official marks, applied only after testing that the standard, or quality, of the metal is right, but the term has also come to embrace the maker's mark. The hall-marking system in Britain has a long history, and it can claim to be the oldest form of consumer protection in the country.

In medieval England, regulation of the goldsmith's craft (the term goldsmith was formerly used without distinction for gold- and silver-smith) was in the hands of the London Goldsmiths' Company. Scotland has never been under their jurisdiction, though after the Act of Union, duties and other London-made laws were applied there. Dublin, likewise, has its own Company, to which Charles I granted a Charter in 1637; in Ireland there was no duty on silver until 1730, and the King's head duty mark there, did not appear until 1807.

The earliest statute concerning gold and silver is that of 1238 A.D., when the standards of fineness were laid down, but the true beginning of hall-marking dates from 1300 A.D., when it was decreed that no piece of silver "was to depart out of the hands of the workers" until it had been assayed (or tested) and marked with the leopard's head. The standard of silver was to be sterling, or 92·5 per cent. pure, which was the same standard as the coinage. At the same time, the "Guardians of the Craft" were instructed to go out among the workers to make sure that the law was enforced, and it was further enacted that "in all good towns of England where there are goldsmiths" the same should apply, and that one of their number should go to London "to seek their sure touch."

The Maker's Mark
In order to supervise the craft, it was obvious that some way had to be found to identify the maker of substandard wares,

and so in 1363 it was commanded that each Master Goldsmith should have his own mark, which had to be registered. In the past, the maker's mark took a variety of forms. Sometimes it was merely a symbol, perhaps his shop sign, or a rebus or pun on his name. Later, initials, often associated with one or more symbols or devices, became common. In 1696, with the introduction of the new higher Britannia Standard, all makers had to re-register their marks, and a completely new style was ordered – the use of the first two letters of the surname. In 1720, when the old sterling standard was restored, so were the old-style marks. Indeed, some makers were using marks of different styles at the same time, so in 1739 all were ordered to re-register with new marks, and from then on most marks took the form of initials of forename and surname, with only an occasional additional symbol such as a crown or a mullet.

The Date Letter

Towards the end of the 15th century, continued complaints about substandard wares resulted in a ruling that the "Keeper of the Touch" – in fact, the Assay Master – should be responsible for maintaining the standard. Probably that led to the date letter system, devised to ascertain the year of assay (and so to trace offending maker and assay-master as well) but by a happy chance also the silver collector's invaluable guide. The first full cycle of date letters in London started with A in 1478, and continued in 20-year cycles (omitting J, and from V to Z) without a break until 1696, when a new series commenced with the new Britannia standard. Since then, each new cycle, differentiated by changing styles of letter and/or shields, has been unbroken.

Outside London, both the length of each cycle and the year of commencement varies considerably, and it is advisable to consult the tables. In addition, slight confusion sometimes arises because assay offices change the year-letter at different times of the year – London changes in May, for instance, Birmingham and Sheffield in June, and Edinburgh in October.

The Leopard's Head

From early documents, it appears that the leopard's head, which was crowned until 1821, was the standard mark, but from 1544, when the lion passant gardant was added to the hall-marks, it became more accurately the authoritative mark of the Goldsmiths' Company, and today it remains as the London town mark. As the Company's mark of authority, it was used by several of the provincial assay offices in addition to their own town mark. In York and Newcastle it was used until those offices were closed in 1857 and 1883 respectively. In Chester it was used until 1838, in Exter until 1777, and it also appeared on the few known pieces of Bristol silver made about 1720-1760. Neither Birmingham nor Sheffield, understandably, used it, and it was seldom struck elsewhere, though various forms of leopard's head, usually debased, were used in East Anglia, in Shrewsbury and even in Jamaica. In 1821, for some unspecified reason, it was deprived of its crown.

The Lion Passant

Sometimes called the sterling mark, the lion passant gardant made its first appearance in 1544, at a period when the coinage, normally of sterling silver, was much debased. It was perhaps struck by the Goldsmiths' Company as an indication that their hall-marked wares were sterling, even if the coinage were not. In 1720 its use was extended to all the existing provincial English assay offices, and it was also adopted at Sheffield and Birmingham when they opened in 1773. In Chester, York and Sheffield the lion passant has always been *gardant*, that is, looking over its shoulder, but elsewhere it changed to being merely *passant* (looking ahead) in London in 1821, in Exeter in 1837, in Newcastle in 1846 and in Birmingham in 1875.

The Britannia Standard

In 1696, so extensive had become the melting and clipping of coinage that the silversmiths were forbidden to use the sterling standard for their wares, but had to use a new higher standard, 95·8 per cent. pure, or another 8 dwts. of silver to the pound troy. New hall-marks were ordered, the "figure of a woman commonly called Britannia" and the lion's head erased (torn off at the neck) replacing the lion passant and the leopard's head crowned. As noted above, a new series of date letters began in March 1697, and makers had to register new marks.

Since the Britannia standard silver was more expensive, the silversmiths began to clamour for the restoration of sterling, though some actually lodged a counter-petition to retain the higher standard, because of advantages in its working (it being softer) and on account of the export trade with Europe. Their pleas were acknowledged by the permission to retain the higher standard alongside sterling when the old standard was restored on June 1, 1720.

The Duty Mark

The price of restoration of sterling in 1720 was a duty of 6d. an ounce on wrought plate. This resulted in the practice known as "duty-dodging" by which some silversmiths avoided paying duty by incorporating pieces of plate bearing hall-marks into a new piece. The duty was removed in 1758, only to be re-imposed, at the same rate, in 1784. Payment of duty was, as before, exacted at the time of assay, but from 1784 until its abolition in 1890, the duty paid was recorded by another hall-mark, the sovereign's head mark. At first, from December 1, 1784, until May 1786, the king's head was incuse, but after that it appeared in cameo. The profiles of George III, George IV and William IV face to the right, the head of Queen Victoria to the left. The duty mark was also struck in Edinburgh from 1784 onwards, in Glasgow from 1819, and in Dublin from 1807. Curiously, some assay offices did not change the punch on the death of the sovereign, and William IV's head sometimes appears on Victorian silver made in Chester, Edinburgh, Glasgow, Newcastle, Sheffield and York as late as 1840 or 1841.

The Duty Drawback Mark, an incuse figure of Britannia standing, is almost certainly the rarest of all hall-marks. It was used for only eight months, from 1st December 1784 until July 1785, on plate exported from England. Being struck after the piece was polished and finished, it was liable to damage it, and was therefore withdrawn, silversmiths simply claiming drawback of duty against shipping notes or invoices.

Outside London

Many of the ancient ordinances and other documents mention goldsmiths outside London, and from time to time various towns have been named as Assay Towns and as Mint Towns. A few survived into the 18th century, and even into the 19th century, as assay towns – Chester, Norwich, Newcastle, Exeter and York, and, apparently, Bristol. For the rest, the wear and tear of the years, changing taste and the consignment of silver to the melting-pot for one reason or another has made the history of the provincial silversmiths of Britain both difficult to unravel and wholly absorbing. Considerable research has brought credible attribution of dozens of different marks to minor centres, and certain identification of many others, such as Barnstaple, Hull, Kings Lynn, Leeds, Plymouth, Taunton, Truro and so on.

The enforcement of the higher Britannia Standard appears to have put an end to one or two of the last centres of silversmithing that survived into the late 17th century. Indeed, the Act of 1696 actually completely ignored even the major provincial centres, and it was not until 1700 that the position was rectified so far as Chester, York, Norwich and Exeter were concerned, and even then Newcastle, a thriving centre of silversmithing right through the 18th century, was ignored until 1701.

Until 1700, only York and, to a lesser degree, Norwich, had any system of date letters, and by then both these towns were almost dormant. Exeter, Newcastle and Chester all continued to be active throughout the 18th century, using as their town marks a triple castle, three keeps and the Arms of the City of Chester respectively.

By the middle of the 18th century, both Birmingham and Sheffield were fast becoming large manufacturing centres for the trade, and largely through the efforts of Matthew Boulton, the Birmingham industrialist, despite the opposition of the London Goldsmiths' Company, an Act of Parliament set up the Birmingham and Sheffield Assay Offices in 1773, Birmingham taking the anchor as its mark, and Sheffield the crown.

Scotland

In 1457 A.D., James II of Scotland proclaimed a standard of 11 ozs. per lb. troy (i.e. 12 ozs.) for wrought silver. At the same time, the practice of striking a Deacon's (or Warden's) mark alongside that of the maker was instituted. In Edinburgh, the town mark, a triple-towered castle, was used from 1485 onwards, but it was 1681 before a date letter system was adopted. Then, too, an Assay Master's mark was substituted for that of the Deacon, until 1759, when it was replaced by the thistle standard mark.

Scotland was not subject to the Britannia Standard, but in 1720, when sterling was restored in England, the standard of silver was raised in Scotland to conform to the English sterling, 11 ozs. 2 dwts. pure per lb. troy, and the 6d. an ounce duty was also imposed.

In 1586, the Edinburgh Goldsmiths had been granted jurisdiction over the craft throughout Scotland, and that was reaffirmed in 1686, at which time there were goldsmiths recorded as working in Glasgow, Aberdeen, Perth, Inverness, Ayr, Banff and Montrose.

Considerable research has been done in recent years on the Scottish craftsmen outside Edinburgh. Glasgow had its own Incorporation of Hammermen by 1536, and in 1681 they too adopted a date letter system. It fell into disuse in the early 18th century, the letters S (perhaps for Sterling or for Scottish), O and E being much used, together with the town mark, a tree with a bird and bell, and a fish below. Glasgow's industrial growth resulted in the formation, in 1819, of an official Assay Office there, and the lion rampant was chosen as the standard mark. The sovereign's head duty mark was also struck, and in 1914 the thistle standard mark was added. The Glasgow Assay Office, which had been running at a loss for some years, was closed in 1964.

Until the rise of Glasgow, Aberdeen was probably the most important trading centre in Scotland outside Edinburgh, and from about 1600 onwards, various marks were used by the silversmiths, usually in the form of the letters AB, ABD or a contracted symbol, with a single or a three castle mark, very like that used in Newcastle. Aberdeen was actually divided into two burghs, Old Aberdeen, where a pike's head mark is associated with one Colline Allen about 1740/1760, and New Aberdeen, where most of the craftsmen worked.

At Banff, where silver was made from about 1680 to 1830, various versions of the name, from B to BANF were struck. At Dundee a pot-of-lilies appeared on silver from about 1625 to 1810, a device based on the town arms, and at Perth one of several marks used during the long history of silversmithing there was the lion and banner of St. John, though during the 18th century the mark changed to a double-headed eagle, the modern town symbol, which was used until about 1850. Inverness boasted silversmiths for some two centuries, from about 1640 to as late as 1880, a dromedary mark sometimes being used alongside the more usual INS abbreviation. Montrose naturally found itself with a rose mark, seen between about 1650 and 1820, at Arbroath there was a portcullis mark taken from the burgh seal, and at Greenock a "green oak" used from about 1760 to 1840 provided a punning mark much like the T over a tun of Taunton. At Wick and Tain the brief names were usually struck in full, Elgin was contracted to Eln or Elg, and used with a mother and child device said to have been based on the story of a widow who took refuge there in 1745. A tall fort mark has been attributed to Forres, a cross to St. Andrews, and another portcullis mark, with S at the base, to Stirling. Possibly PH stands for Peterhead, where a key mark may also have been used, but much work still remains to be done, not only in identifying town marks but in establishing where some of the itinerant craftsmen worked.

Ireland

Of all the gold and silversmiths in Britain, Ireland's have undoubtedly the longest unbroken history, dating back to the Bronze Age craftsmen. In the Middle Ages, the Dublin goldsmiths were a substantial guild, and in 1555 they were granted a Charter, which was followed by a Royal Charter in 1637. This prescribed the sterling standard, with the harp crowned as the standard mark, superseding a previous, but apparently unenforced, lion, harp and castle. In 1638 a date letter system began, but the series used and even the time each letter was used was somewhat haphazard, and in 1730, when a duty of 6d. an ounce was imposed and the duty paid indicated by a figure of Hibernia, often the date letter was omitted altogether. The Hibernia mark somewhat resembles the Britannia on English silver (as in Scotland, there was no era of Britannia silver in Ireland). Officially, it was struck as a tax "for the encouragement of tillage", but in 1806 Irish silver was struck with the king's head duty mark as well, so that the Hibernia tended to become the Dublin Assay Office mark.

There are very full lists of makers registered with the Dublin Goldsmiths' Company, so that identification of most makers' marks from 1637 onwards is possible. From 1784 onwards, many provincial Irish silversmiths were also registered at Dublin, and not a few names are recorded in the local records of Cork, Youghal, Galway, and Limerick.

Though no assay offices were authorised outside Dublin (except for one at Waterford to deal with watch cases in 1784 and never apparently put to use) there were guilds in provincial cities. At Cork, goldsmiths were incorporated with other trades in 1656, but most of their records were destroyed in 1891 in a fire at the Courthouse. The names and marks of many Cork goldsmiths are, however, known from the mid-17th century until the beginning of Queen Victoria's reign. A castle, sometimes accompanied by a ship, was used until the early 18th century, when most silversmiths appear to have used their own name punch and the word Sterling or Starling. In Limerick, too, a castle mark was used, from about 1660 to 1710, but after that Sterling in one form or another was usual. Youghal was also identified by a ship mark, a local yawl, and maritime connections were also indicated by the anchor of Galway, used from about 1660 to 1730.

In Ireland, as in England and Scotland, and in the British territories overseas, research goes on, and much still remains to be done in identifying both town marks and maker's marks, and in adding to the small but increasing knowledge of silversmithing in the provinces.

The Use and Abuse of Hall-marks

Obviously hall-marks are a godsend to the silver collector, an invaluable guide to the quality of the metal, the date, the provenance and the maker. But too much reliance on hall-marks, taken at their face value without reference to the piece on which they appear, can be dangerous, and may even lay the collector open to the wiles of the forger.

In reading hall-marks, care should be taken in looking at the shape of the shields, or outlines of the punch; the style of the town mark and the standard mark; the style of the date letter and the actual appearance and crispness of the marks, as well as their position on the piece. Hall-marks are struck with very carefully made dies that leave a sharp impression when they are first punched, and even long years of wear will not usually leave a "soft" appearance which is one of the signs of the faker, who is not usually prepared to spend the time and money making high-grade dies. This is not to say that all "rubbed" marks are suspect, though one should immediately be suspicious of fairly good Britannia marks with very rubbed maker's marks and date letter. Incidentally, very few makers' marks are as crisply struck as the official hall-marks. The placing of the marks is also an important guide: a London-made tankard and cover of 17th century date would have the

14

marks to the right of the handle, near the rim, and another set across the top of the flat cap cover. A mid-18th century one would have the marks on the base. Spoons and forks until 1780 had "bottom marks" near the bowl end, after that they were placed near the end of the stem.

Not all good antique silver bears full hall-marks. Some is completely unmarked, some bears the maker's mark only, struck once or several times. In itself, the maker's mark is not a guarantee of quality, though the assay office at the period could easily have traced the maker from their registers, and many pieces made to special order were not sent for assay due to an interpretation of the law which suggested that only goods "set for sale" were liable for assay. In some instances, the assay offices themselves made errors, omitting, say, the date letter and striking the lion passant twice. But on a fully marked piece, one would expect full marks on the main section, and at least the maker's mark and usually also the lion passant on minor parts, such as the lid of a tankard or coffee pot.

The status of the hall-mark led to many imitations of it, first among the pewterers and later, in the mid-18th century, by the makers of plated goods. Many marks on Old Sheffield Plate, on close-plated wares and, from about 1860, on electro-plated wares, somewhat resemble silver marks. The imitation marks on Sheffield fused plate in the later 18th century led to restrictions on the type of mark that the platers could register, and most Sheffield Plate marks after 1784 include the maker's full name. Electro-plated wares sometimes also carry hall-mark-like stamps, but often the letters EP, EPNS or EPBM for nickel plated, and Britannia metal wares can be detected, and careful examination of the piece will usually reveal the base metal core.

Hall-marking Today

In England, only three Assay Offices remain – London, Birmingham and Sheffield. In Scotland there is now only Edinburgh, while in the Republic of Ireland, Dublin still administers the law there. All silver wares, and most gold-wares are obliged to be sent for assay and hall-marking, and so too are imported silver and gold, which are struck with special import marks.

From time to time, special marks are authorised for short

periods, and it seems likely that pieces bearing these commemorative hall-marks will be of especial interest to the collectors of the future. In England and Scotland, from 1933 to 1935, a Jubilee Mark, showing the profile heads of King George V and Queen Mary, commemorated their Silver Jubilee, and the profile of Queen Elizabeth II was struck on all silver made in England and Scotland in 1952 and 1953 to mark her Coronation. In Ireland in 1966 a torch mark was struck on silver and gold in 1966 to commemorate the fiftieth anniversary of the October Rising.

THE MARKS ON GOLD

Most of the Statutes regulating hall-marking applied equally to gold, and the marks used were the same as those on silver until 1798, though the standard was changed from time to time. In 1477 it was reduced from 19·2 ct. to 18 ct., but in 1575 it was raised to 22 ct., at which it remained until 1798, being marked with the maker's mark, the lion passant, the assay office mark and the date letter with the sovereign's head duty mark also from 1784. A major change in gold marking in England occurred in 1798, when both 18 ct. and 22 ct. gold were permitted, and were indicated by the relevant figures and by a crown, which replaced the lion passant standard mark. In 1854 three lower standards were introduced, and these were indicated by the carat number plus the value in decimals: 9 with ·375; 12 with ·5 and 15 with ·625. In 1931, 12 ct. and 15 ct. were replaced by 14 ct. (·585) and the crown mark since 1854 has been reserved for the higher 18 ct. and 22 ct. standards. In Sheffield, which obtained a licence to assay goldwares in 1903, the gold mark is a rose (to avoid confusion with the town mark used on silver). In Edinburgh, the Thistle replaces the crown on 18 ct. and 22 ct. gold, while in Glasgow, until its closure in 1964, the Lion Rampant appeared on all permitted standards.

Ireland from 1784 had three standards for gold – 22 ct. marked with the figures and with the crowned harp and Hibernia; 20 ct. indicated by figures and with a plume of feathers also: and 18 ct. with the figures and a unicorn's head. The crowned harp was omitted from the lower standard goldwares, and on jewellery.

Year	Letter	Mark	Lion	
1544				
1545				Henry VIII
				1547 Edward VI
				1553 Mary
1546				
1547				
1548				
1549				
1550				
1551				
1552				
1553				
1554				
1555				
1556				
1557				

B

LONDON

Eliz. I	1558	1564	1572	
	1559	1565	1573	
	1560	1566	1574	
	1561	1567	1575	
	1562	1568	1576	
	1563	1569	1577	
		1570		
		1571		

Eliz. I	1578	1585	1592	
	1579	1586	1593	
	1580	1587	1594	
	1581	1588	1595	
	1582	1589	1596	
	1583	1590	1597	
	1584	1591		

Eliz. I 1603 James I	1598	1605	1613	
	1599	1606	1614	
	1600	1607	1615	
	1601	1608	1616	
	1602	1609	1617	
	1603	1610		
	1604	1611		
		1612		

LONDON

1618	a	1625	h	1633	q
1619	b	1626	i	1634	r
1620	c	1627	k	1635	s
1621	d	1628	l	1636	t
1622	e	1629	m	1637	v
1623	f	1630	n		
1624	g	1631	o		
		1632	p		

James I
1625
Charles I

1638	a	1645	B	1652	P
1639	B	1646	J	1653	Q
1640	C	1647	R	1654	R
1641	D	1648	P	1655	S
1642	E	1649	N	1656	T
1643	ff	1650	R	1657	V
1644	H	1651	O		

Charles I
1649
Charles II

1658	A	1665	H	1672	P P
1659	B	1666	J	1673	Q
1660	C	1667	K	1674	R
1661	D	1668	L	1675	S
1662	E	1669	M	1676	T
1663	F	1670	N	1677	U
1664	G	1671	O		

Charles II

19

LONDON

Frame 1

Charles II
1685 James II
1689 Wm. & My.
1694 William III

1678		1683	🛡f	1691	🛡o	
1679		1684	🛡g	1692	🛡p	
1680		1685	🛡h	1693	🛡q	
1681		1686	🛡i	1694	🛡r	
1682		1687	🛡k	1695	🛡s	
		1688	🛡l	1696	🛡t	
		1689	🛡m	1697	🛡t	
		1690	🛡n			

Frame 2

William III
1702 Anne
1714 George I

1697		1702		1710	
1698		1703		1711	
1699		1704		1712	
1700		1705		1713	
1701		1706		1714	
		1707		1715	
		1708			
		1709			

Frame 3

George I

1716	Ⓐ	1721	🛡F	
1717	Ⓑ	1722	🛡G	
1718	Ⓒ	1723	🛡H	
1719	Ⓓ	1724	🛡I	
1720	Ⓔ	1725	🛡K	

Though not compulsory after 1720, the Britannia Standard was sometimes used as an alternative standard. The identifying marks are to be found between 1720 and the present time. A piece of Britannia Silver assayed in 1721 would therefore carry the marks:

See also the notes in frame 1 on page 23.

20

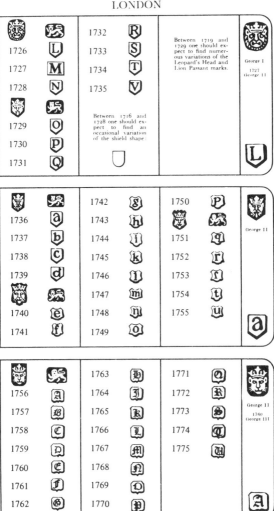

1726	L	1732	R	Between 1719 and 1729 one should expect to find numerous variations of the Leopard's Head and Lion Passant marks.		George I 1727 George II	
1727	M	1733	S				
1728	N	1734	T				
1729	O	1735	V				
1730	P		Between 1716 and 1728 one should expect to find an occasional variation of the shield shape:			L	
1731	Q						

1736	a	1742	g	1750	P	George II	
1737	b	1743	h	1751	q		
1738	c	1744	i	1752	r		
1739	d	1745	k	1753	s		
1740	e	1746	l	1754	t		
1741	f	1747	m	1755	u	a	
		1748	n				
		1749	o				

1756	A	1763	H	1771	Q	George II 1760 George III	
1757	B	1764	J	1772	R		
1758	C	1765	K	1773	S		
1759	D	1766	L	1774	T		
1760	E	1767	M	1775	U		
1761	F	1768	N				
1762	G	1769	O			a	
		1770	P				

LONDON

George III	1776	**a**	1783	**h**	1791	**q**
	1777	**b**	1784	**i**	1792	**r**
	1778	**c**	1785	**k**	1793	**s**
	1779	**d**	1786	**l**	1794	**t**
	1780	**e**	1787	**m**	1795	**u**
	1781	**f**	1788	**n**		
	1782	**g**	1789	**o**		
			1790	**p**		

An alternative shield may be found.

George III	1796	**A**	1803	**H**	1811	**Q**
	1797	**B**	1804	**I**	1812	**R**
	1798	**C**	1805	**K**	1813	**S**
	1799	**D**	1806	**L**	1814	**T**
	1800	**E**	1807	**M**	1815	**U**
	1801	**F**	1808	**N**		
	1802	**G**	1809	**O**		
			1810	**P**		

An alternative shield may be found.

George III / 1820 George IV / 1830 William IV	1816	**a**	1821	**f**	1828	**n**
	1817	**b**	1822	**g**	1829	**o**
	1818	**c**	1823	**h**	1830	**p**
	1819	**d**	1824	**i**	1831	**q**
	1820	**e**	1825	**k**	1832	**r**
			1826	**l**	1833	**s**
			1827	**m**	1834	**t**
					1835	**u**

	1843	1851		William IV
1836	1844	1852		1837 Victoria
1837	1845	1853		
1838	1846	1854		
1839	1847	1855		
1840	1848	An alternative shield may be found.		
1841	1849			
1842	1850			

	1863	1871		Victoria
1856	1864	1872		
1857	1865	1873		
1858	1866	1874		
1859	1867	1875		
1860	1868	An alternative shield may be found.		
1861	1869			
1862	1870			

	1883		1891	Victoria
1876	1884		1892	
1877	1885		1893	
1878	1886		1894	
1879	1887		1895	
1880	1888			
1881	1889			
1882	1890			

Victoria / 1901 Ewd. VII / 1910 George V	1896 **a**	1903 **h**	1911 **q**
	1897 **b**	1904 **i**	1912 **r**
	1898 **c**	1905 **k**	1913 **s**
	1899 **d**	1906 **l**	1914 **t**
	1900 **e**	1907 **m**	1915 **u**
	1901 **f**	1908 **n**	
	1902 **g**	1909 **o**	
		1910 **p**	

George V	1916 **a**	1923 **h**	1931 **q**
	1917 **b**	1924 **i**	1932 **r**
	1918 **c**	1925 **k**	1933 **s**
	1919 **d**	1926 **l**	1934 **t**
	1920 **e**	1927 **m**	1935 **u**
	1921 **f**	1928 **n**	The Britannia Standard Marks for 1927
	1922 **g**	1929 **o**	
		1930 **p**	

1936 Ewd. VIII / 1936 George VI / 1952 Eliz. II	1936 **A**	1943 **H**	1951 **Q**
	1937 **B**	1944 **I**	1952 **R**
	1938 **C**	1945 **K**	1953 **S**
	1939 **D**	1946 **L**	1954
	1940 **E**	1947 **M**	1955 **U**
	1941 **F**	1948 **N**	**T**
	1942 **G**	1949 **O**	
		1950 **P**	

🦁	🐆	1963	**h**	1971	**q**	🐆
1956	**a**	1964	**i**	1972	**r**	Eliz. II
1957	**b**	1965	**k**			
1958	**c**	1966	**l**			
1959	**d**	1967	**m**			
1960	**e**	1968	**n**			
1961	**f**	1969	**o**			
1962	**g**	1970	**p**			**a**

BIRMINGHAM

⚓ George III	🦁	⚓	1781	I	1790	S
	1773	A	1782	K	1791	T
	1774	B	1783	L	1792	U
	1775	C	1784	M 👤	1793	V
	1776	D	1785	N	1794	W
	1777	E	1786	O 👤	1795	X
	1778	F	1787	P	1796	Y
	1779	G	1788	Q	1797	Z
A	1780	H	1789	R	July '97 to March '8o. The King's Head is duplicated.	

⚓ George III 1820 George IV	🦁	⚓	👤	1806	i	1815	r
	1798	a	1807	j	1816	s
	1799	b	1808	k	1817	t
	1800	c	1809	l 👤	1818	u
	1801	d	1810	m	1819	v
	1802	e	1811	n	1820	w
	1803	f	1812	o	1821	x
	1804	g	1813	p	1822	y
a	1805	h	1814	q	1823	z

⚓ George IV 1830 William IV 1837 Victoria	🦁	⚓	👤	1832	J	1841	S
	1824	A	1833	K	1842	T
	1825	B	1834	L 👤	1843	U
	1826	C	1835	M	1844	V
	1827	D	1836	N	1845	W
	1828	E	1837	O	1846	X
	1829	F	1838	P 👤	1847	Y
	1830	G	1839	Q	1848	Z
A	1831	H 👤	1840	R		

BIRMINGHAM

🦁⚓👑		🦁⚓👑	⚓
	1858 **J**		Victoria
1849 **A**	1859 **K**	1867 **S**	
1850 **B**	1860 **L**	1868 **T**	
1851 **C**	1861 **M**	1869 **U**	
1852 **D**	1862 **N**	1870 **V**	
1853 **E**	1863 **O**	1871 **W**	
1854 **F**	1864 **P**	1872 **X**	**A**
1855 **G**	1865 **Q**	1873 **Y**	
1856 **H**	1866 **R**	1874 **Z**	
1857 **I**			

🦁⚓👑	🦁⚓👑		⚓
		1891 **r**	Victoria
1875 **a**	1883 **i**	1892 **s**	
1876 **b**	1884 **k**	1893 **t**	
1877 **c**	1885 **l**	1894 **u**	
1878 **d**	1886 **m**	1895 **v**	
1879 **e**	1887 **n**	1896 **w**	
1880 **f**	1888 **o**	1897 **x**	
1881 **g**	1889 **p**	1898 **y**	
1882 **h**	1890 **q**	1899 **z**	**a**

BIRMINGHAM

Victoria / 1901 Ewd. VII / 1910 George V	1900	a	1908	i	1917	S
	1901	b	1909	k		(anchor / lion)
	1902	c	1910	l	1918	t
	1903	d	1911	m	1919	u
	1904	e	1912	n	1920	v
	1905	f	1913	o	1921	w
	1906	g	1914	p	1922	x
	1907	h	1915	q	1923	y
			1916	r	1924	z

George V / 1936 Ewd. VIII	1925	A	1933	J	1940	Q
	1926	B	1934	K	1941	R
	1927	C	1935	L	1942	S
	1928	D	(anchor / lion)		1943	T
	1929	E	1936	M	1944	U
	1930	F	1937	N	1945	V
	1931	G	1938	O	1946	W
	1932	H	1939	P	1947	X
					1948	Y
					1949	Z

BIRMINGHAM

⚓	🦁	⚓	🦁	1960	*L*	⚓	
1950	*A*	1954	*E*	1961	*M*	George VI	
1951	*B*	1955	*F*	1962	*N*	1952 Eliz. II	
⚓ 🦁 ○		1956	*G*	1963	*O*		
1952	*C*	1957	*H*	1964	*P*		
1953	*D*	1958	*J*	1965	*2*		
		1959	*K*			*A*	

⚓	🦁					⚓
1966	*R*					Eliz. II
1967	*S*					
1968	*T*					
1969	*U*					
1970	*V*					
1971	*W*					*R*

STERLING Charles II 1685 James II 1689 Wm. & My. 1694 William III	1680		1690	1690 to 1700 STERLING

William III 1702 Anne 1714 George I A	1701	A	1709	I	1718	S
	1702	B	1710	K	1719	T
	1703	C	1711	L	1720	U
	1704	D	1712	M	1721	V
	1705	E	1713	N	1722	W
	1706	F	1714	O	1723	X
	1707	G	1715	P	1724	Y
	1708	H	1716	Q	1725	Z
			1717	R		

George I 1727 George II A	1726	A	1734	J	1743	J
	1727	B	1735	K	1744	J
	1728	C	1736	L	1745	U
	1729	D	1737	M	1746	V
	1730	E	1738	N	1747	W
	1731	F	1739	O	1748	X
	1732	G	1740	P	1749	Y
	1733	K	1741	Q	1750	Z
			1742	R		

1751	a	1759	i	1768	S	
1752	b	1760	k	1769	T	
1753	c	1761	l	1770	U	
1754	d	1762	m	1771	U	George II
1755	e	1763	n	1772	V	1760 George III
1756	f	1764	o	1773	W	
1757	G	1765	P	1774	X	
1758	h	1766	Q	1775	Y	a
		1767	R			

1776	a	1782	g	1789	o	
1777	b	1783	h	1790	p	
1778	c	1784	i	1791	q	George III
1779	d	1785	k	1792	r	
1780	e	1786	l	1793	s	
1781	f	1787	m	1794	t	
		1788	n	1795	u	
				1796	v	a

1797	A	1803	G	1811	P	
1798	B	1804	H	1812	Q	
1799	C	1805	I	1813	R	
1800	D	1806	K	1814	S	George III
1801	E	1807	L	1815	T	
1802	F	1808	M	1816	U	
		1809	N	1817	V	
		1810	O			A

31

		1824	**F**	1833	**P**
	1818 **A**	1825	**G**	1834	**Q**
	1819 **B**	1826	**H**	1835	**R**
George III	1820 **C**	1827	**I**	1836	**S**
1820 George IV	1821 **D**	1828	**K**	1837	**T**
1830 William IV	1822 **D**	1829	**L**	1838	**U**
1837 Victoria				1830	
	1831				
A	1823 **E**	1832	**O**		

		1847	**J**	1856	**S**
Victoria	1839 **A**	1848	**K**	1857	**T**
	1840 **B**	1849	**L**	1858	**U**
	1841 **C**	1850	**M**	1859	**V**
	1842 **D**	1851	**N**	1860	**W**
	1843 **E**	1852	**O**	1861	**X**
	1844 **F**	1853	**P**	1862	**Y**
A	1845 **G**	1854	**Q**	1863	**Z**
	1846 **H**	1855	**R**		

		1871	**h**	1879	**q**
Victoria	1864 **a**	1872	**i**	1880	**r**
	1865 **b**	1873	**k**	1881	**s**
	1866 **c**	1874	**l**	1882	**t**
	1867 **d**	1875	**m**	1883	**u**
	1868 **e**	1876	**n**		
	1869 **f**	1877	**o**		
a	1870 **g**	1878	**p**		

CHESTER

1884 **A**	1890 **G**	1897 **O**		Victoria
1885 **B**	1891 **H**	1898 **P**		
1886 **C**	1892 **I**	1899 **Q**		
1887 **D**	1893 **K**	1900 **R**		
1888 **E**	1894 **L**	An alternative sterling mark used since 1839.		
1889 **F**	1895 **M**	An alternative date letter shield used since 1900.		**A**
	1896 **N**			

1901 **A**	1908 **H**	1917 **R**	Edw. VII
1902 **B**	1909 **J**	1918 **S**	1910 George V
1903 **C**	1910 **K**	1919 **T**	
1904 **D**	1911 **L**	1920 **U**	
1905 **E**	1912 **M**	1921 **V**	
1906 **F**	1913 **N**	1922 **W**	
1907 **G**	1914 **O**	1923 **X**	
	1915 **P**	1924 **Y**	
	1916 **Q**	1925 **Z**	**A**

1926 **a**	1933 **h**	1940 **P**	George V
1927 **B**	1934 **I**	1941 **Q**	1936 Edw. VIII
1928 **C**	1935 **R**	1942 **R**	1936 George VI
1929 **D**	1936	1943 **S**	
1930 **E**	1936 **u**	1944 **t**	
1931 **ff**	1937 **w**	1945 **u**	
1932 **G**	1938 **n**	1946 **v**	
	1939 **o**	1947 **w**	**a**

CHESTER

George VI / 1952 Eliz. II	1948	1954	D	1961	L
	1949	1955	E	1962	M
	1950	1956	F	In August of 1962 the Chester Assay Office closed.	
	1951	1957	G		
	1952	1958	H		
	1953	1959	J		
		1960	K		

1638	A	1645	H	1652	P
1639	B	1646	I	1653	Q
1640	C	1647	K	1654	R
1641	D	1648	L	1655	S
1642	E	1649	M	1656	T
1643	F	1650	N	1657	U
1644	G	1651	O		

Charles I
1649 Charles II

1658	a	1665	h	1672	p
1659	b	1666	i	1673	q
1660	c	1667	k	1674	r
1661	d	1668	l	1675	s
1662	e	1669	m	1676	t
1663	f	1670	n	1677	u
1664	g	1671	o		

Charles II

1678	A	1688-93	h	1704	R
1679	B	1694-5	k	1706-7	S
1680	C	1696-8	l	1708-9	T
1681	D	1699	M	1710-11	U
1682	E	1700	N	1712-13	W
1683-4	F	1701	D	1714	X
1685-7	G	1702	P	1715	P
		1703	Q	1716	Z

Charles II
1685 James II
1689 Wm. & My.
1694 William III
1702 Anne
1714 George I

35

(harp marks)	(harp)	1726	𝕲	1736	𝕺
George I	1717	𝕬	1727	𝕳	1737	𝕽
1727 George II	1718	𝕭	1728	𝕴	1738	𝕾
	1719	𝕮	1729	𝕶	1739	𝕿
	(harp) 1720	𝔸	1730	𝕷	1740	𝖀 𝖀
(a)	1721	𝔹	(harp) 1731	𝕰	1741-2	𝖂 𝖂
	1722	ℂ	1732	𝕸	1743-4	𝖃
	1723	𝔻	1733	𝕹	1745	𝖄
	1724	𝔼	1734	𝕺	1746	𝖅
	1725	𝔽	1735	𝕻	An alternative Crowned Harp found between 1739 and 1748.	

(harp mark)	(Hibernia)	(harp)	1757	𝕀	1766	𝕊
	1747	𝔸	1758	𝕂	(harp)	
(Hibernia)			1759	𝕃	1767	𝕋
George II	1748	𝔹	(harp)		1768	𝕌
1760 George III	1749	ℂ	1760	𝕄	1769	𝕎
	1750	𝔻	1761	ℕ	1770	𝕏
	1751	𝔼 𝔼	1762	𝕆	1771	𝕐
	1752	𝔽	1763	ℙ	1772	ℤ
	1753	𝔾	1764	ℚ	An alternative Hibernia found between 1752 and 1754.	
(A)	1754	ℍ	1765	ℝ	(Hibernia)	

DUBLIN

(harp mark)	(crowned harp)	1781	Ⓘ	1790	Ⓢ	(crowned harp)
1773	Ⓐ	1782	Ⓚ	1791	Ⓣ	
1774	Ⓑ	1783	Ⓛ	1792	Ⓤ	(Hibernia mark)
1775	Ⓒ	1784	Ⓜ	(Hibernia mark)	(crowned harp)	George III
(harp mark)	(crowned harp)	1785	Ⓝ	1793	Ⓦ	
1776	Ⓓ	1786	Ⓞ	1794	Ⓧ	Ⓐ
1777	Ⓔ	(Hibernia mark)	(crowned harp)	1795	Ⓨ	
1778	Ⓕ	1787	Ⓟ	1796	Ⓩ	
1779	Ⓖ	1788	Ⓠ			
1780	Ⓗ	1789	Ⓡ			

(Hibernia mark)	(crowned harp)	1806	Ⓚ	1815	Ⓣ	(crowned harp)
1797	Ⓐ	1807	Ⓛ (Hibernia)	1816	Ⓤ	
1798	Ⓑ	1808	Ⓜ	1817	Ⓦ	(Hibernia mark)
1799	Ⓒ	1809	Ⓝ (Hibernia)	1818	Ⓧ	George III
1800	Ⓓ	(Hibernia) (crowned harp) (Hibernia)		1819	Ⓨ	1820 George IV
1801	Ⓔ	1810	Ⓞ	1820	Ⓩ	
1802	Ⓕ	1811	Ⓟ			
1803	Ⓖ	1812	Ⓠ			
1804	Ⓗ	1813	Ⓡ			
1805	Ⓘ	1814	Ⓢ			Ⓐ

	1821	Ⓐ	🦁	🛡	👤
	1822	Ⓑ			👤
	1823	Ⓒ			
	1824	Ⓓ			
1820 George IV	1825	Ⓔ ⓔ			
1830 William IV	1826	Ⓕ			
1837 Victoria	1827	Ⓖ	🦁	🛡	👤
	1828	Ⓗ	🦁	🛡	👤
	1829	Ⓘ	🦁	🛡	👤
	1830	Ⓚ	🦁	🛡	👤
	1831	Ⓛ	🦁	🛡	👤
	1832	Ⓜ			
	1833	Ⓝ	🦁	🛡	
	1834	Ⓞ	🦁	🛡	👤
	1835	Ⓟ			
	1836	Ⓠ			
	1837	Ⓡ	🦁	🛡	👤
	1838	Ⓢ			👤
	1839	Ⓣ	🦁	🛡	
	1840	Ⓤ			
	1841	Ⓥ			
	1842	Ⓦ	🦁	🛡	
	1843	Ⓧ			
	1844	Ⓨ	🦁	🛡	
Ⓐ	1845	Ⓩ	🦁		🛡

38

1846	à	1855	k	1864	t		
1847	b	1856	l	1865	u	Victoria	
1848	c	1857	m	1866	v		
1849	d	1858	n	1867	w		
1850	e	1859	o	1868	x	à	
1851	ff	1860	p	1869	y		
1852	gg	1861	q	1870	z		
1853	hh	1862	r				
1854	j	1863	s				

1871	A	1880	K	1890	U	Victoria	
1872	B	1881	L	1891	V		
1873	C	1882	M	1892	W		
1874	D	1883	N	1893	X		
1875	E	1884	O	1894	Y		
1876	F	1885	P	1895	Z		
1877	G	1886	Q				
1878	H	1887	R				
1879	I	1888	S			A	
		1889	T				

DUBLIN

Victoria 1901 Ewd. VII 1910 George V	🏷	🏷	1902	**G**	1909	**O**
	1896	**A**	1903	**H**	1910	**P**
	1897	**B**	1904	**I**	1911	**Q**
	1898	**C**	1905	**K**	1912	**R**
	1899	**D**	1906	**L**	1913	**S**
🏷	1900	**E**	1907	**M**	1914	**T**
	1901	**F**	1908	**N**	1915	**U**

George V 1936 Ewd. VIII 1936 George VI	🏷	🏷	1925	**B**	1935	**T**
	1916	**A**	1926	**l**	1936	**u**
	1917	**b**	1927	**m**	🏷	🏷
	1918	**C**	1928	**n**	1937	**v**
	1919	**D**	1929	**O**	1938	**w**
	1920	**e**	1930	**P**	1939	**x**
	1921	**F**	1931	**P**	1940	**y**
	1922	**S**	1932	**Q**	1941	**Z**
	1923	**h**	1933	**R**		
🏷	1924	**i**	1934	**S**		

DUBLIN

🏵	🏵	1951	J	1960	S		🏵
1942	A	1952	K	1961	T		🏵
1943	B	1953	L	1962	U		George VI
1944	C	1954	M	1963	V		1952 Eliz. II
1945	D	🏵 🏵		1964	W		
1946	E	1955	N	1965	X		
1947	F	1956	O	🏵 🏵 🏵			**A**
1948	G	1957	P	1966	Y		
1949	H	1958	Q	🏵 🏵			
1950	I	1959	R	1967	Z		

🏵 🏵				🏵
1968	ⓐ			🏵
1969	ⓑ			Eliz. II
1970	ⓒ			
1971	ⓓ			
1972	ⓔ			
1973	ⓕ			
				ⓐ

41

EDINBURGH

Edward VI	1552		1611		1643
1553 Mary	1563	IC	1617	IL	1644
1558 Eliz. I	1570		1617	G	1649	GC
1603 James I	1576	A	1613-21		1651
1625 Charles I	1585	M	1616-35	G	1660	B
1649 Charles II	1590		1633	A	1665	I·S
	1591		1637	I	1669	
	1591-4	VC	1640	T	1663-81	E
	1596	H	1642	IF	1675	
	1609	R				

1685 James II		B	1689	i		P
1689 Wm. & My.	1681	a	1690	k	1698	S
1694 William III		B	1691	l	1699	t
1702 Anne	1682	b	1692	m	1700	v
	1683	c	1693	n	1701	w
	1684	d	1694	o		
	1685	e	1695	p	1702	r
	1686	f	1696	q	1703	y
	1687	g	1697	r	1704	z
a	1688	h				

42

EDINBURGH

🏰	💟	1713	I	1721	R	🐻🏰
1705	A	🏰	EP	1722	S	Anne
1706	B	1714	K	1723	T	1714 George I
🏰	EP	1715	L	1724	U	1727 George II
1707	C	1716	M	1725	V	
1708	D	1717	N	1726	W	
1709	E	🏰	EP	1727	X	
1710	F	1718	O	1728	Y	A
1711	G	1719	P	1729	Z	
🏰	EP	🏰	EP			
1712	H	1720	q			

🏰	AU	1739	K	1746	R	🏰
1730	A	🏰	GED	🏰	HG	George II
1731	B	1740	L	1747	S	
1732	C	1741	M	1748	J	
1733	D	🏰	EL	1749	U	
1734	E	1742	N	1750	U	
1735	F	1743	O	1751	W	
1736	G	🏰	HG	1752	X	
1737	H	1744	P	1753	Y	
1738	J	1745	2	1754	Z	A

EDINBURGH

George II / 1760 George III	HG		1763		1771	R
	1755	A	1764	k	1772	S
	1756	B	1765	L	1773	T
	1757	C	1766	M	1774	U
	1758	D	1767	N	1775	V
	1759	E	1768	O	1776	X
	1760	F	1769	P	1777	Y
	1761	G	1770	Q	1778	Z
	1762	H			1779	U

Alternative town marks sometimes found around 1771.

George III			1789	IJ	1798	S
	1780	A	1790	K	1799	T
	1781	B	1791	L	1800	U
	1782	C	1792	M	1801	V
	1783	D	1793	N		
	1784	E	1794	O	1802	W
	1785	F	1795	P	1803	X
	1786	G	1796	Q	1804	Y
	1787	G			1805	Z
A	1788	H	1797	R		

44

🏰	🌸	1814	i	🏰	🌸		🏰
1806	a 👤	1815	j	1824	s 👤		George III
1807	b	1816	k	1825	t		1820 George IV
1808	c	1817	l	🏰	🌸		1830 William IV
🏰	🌸	1818	m	1826	u 👤		
1809	d 👤	1819	n	1827	v		
1810	e	🏰	🌸	1828	w		a
1811	f	1820	o 👤	1829	x		
1812	g	1821	p	1830	y		
🏰	🌸	1822	q	1831	z		
1813	h 👤	1823	r				

🏰	🌸	1841	𝕶 👤	1851	𝖀		🏰
1832	𝕬 👤	1842	𝕷	1852	𝖁		William IV
1833	𝕭	1843	𝕸	1853	𝖂		1837 Victoria
1834	𝕮	1844	𝕹	1854	𝖃		
1835	𝕯	1845	𝕺	1855	𝖄		
1836	𝕰	1846	𝕻	1856	𝖅		
1837	𝕱	1847	𝕼				
1838	𝕲	1848	𝕽				
1839	𝕳	1849	𝕾				
1840	𝕵	1850	𝕿				𝕬

(castle) (thistle) (head)	1865 Ⓘ	1874 Ⓢ	
Victoria 1857 Ⓐ	1866 Ⓚ	(castle) (thistle) (head)	
1858 Ⓑ	1867 Ⓛ	1875 Ⓣ	
1859 Ⓒ	1868 Ⓜ	1876 Ⓤ	
1860 Ⓓ	1869 Ⓝ	1877 Ⓥ	
Ⓐ 1861 Ⓔ	1870 Ⓞ	1878 Ⓦ	
1862 Ⓕ	1871 Ⓟ	1879 Ⓧ	
1863 Ⓖ	1872 Ⓠ	1880 Ⓨ	
1864 Ⓗ	1873 Ⓡ	1881 Ⓩ	

(castle) (thistle) (head)	(castle) (thistle) (head)	1898 ⓣ	
Victoria 1901 Ewd. VII 1882 ⓐ	1890 ⓘ	1899 ⓢ	
1883 ⓑ	1891 ⓚ	1900 ⓣ	
1884 ⓒ	1892 ⓛ	1901 ⓥ	
1885 ⓓ	1893 ⓜ	1902 ⓜ	
1886 ⓔ	1894 ⓝ	1903 ⓡ	
1887 ⓕ	1895 ⓞ	1904 ⓨ	
1888 ⓖ	1896 ⓟ	1905 ③	
ⓐ 1889 ⓗ	1897 ⓠ		

EDINBURGH

Year	Mark	Year	Mark	Year	Mark	Sovereign
		1914	I			Ewd. VII
1906	A	1915	K	1923	S	1910 George V
1907	B	1916	L	1924	T	
1908	C	1917	M	1925	U	
1909	D	1918	N	1926	V	
1910	E	1919	O	1927	W	A
1911	F	1920	P	1928	X	
1912	G	1921	Q	1929	Y	
1913	H	1922	R	1930	Z	

Year	Mark	Year	Mark	Year	Mark	Sovereign
1931	A	1939	J	1948	S	Ewd. VIII
1932	B	1940	K	1949	T	1936 George VI
1933	C	1941	L	1950	U	1952 Eliz. II
1934	D	1942	M	1951	V	
1935	E	1943	N	1952	W	
1936	F	1944	O	1953	X	
1937	G	1945	P	1954	Y	
1938	H	1946	Q	1955	Z	A
		1947	R			

47

Eliz. II	1956	A	1965	k
	1957	B	1966	l
	1958	C	1967	m
	1959	D	1968	n
	1960	E	1969	o
A	1961	F	1970	p
	1962	G	1971	q
	1963	H		
	1964	λ		

X **IONS**			**X**
1570			**IONS**
	1585 1630		Eliz. I
I **n**			1603 James I
1571	1635 1675	1690	1625 Charles I
			1649 Charles II
1575	1680		1685 James II
		1698	1689 Wm. & My.
1580			1694 William III

	1709 **U**	1718 **S**	
1701 **A**	1710 **K**	1719 **T**	
1702 **B**	1711 **L**	1720 **V**	Anne
1703 **C**	1712 **M**		1714 George I
1704 **D**	1713 **N**	1721 **W**	
1705 **E**	1714 **O**	1722 **X**	
1706 **F**	1715 **P**	1723 **Y**	
1707 **G**	1716 **Q**	1724 **Z**	
1708 **H**	1717 **R**		**A**

		1733	i	1741	r
	1725 a	1734	k	1742	s
	1726 b	1735	l	1743	t
	1727 c	1736	m	1744	u
George I	1728 d	1737	n	1745	w
1727 George II	1729 e	1738	o	1746	x
	1730 f	1739	p	1747	y
	1731 g	1740	q	1748	z
a	1732 h				

		1757	I	1765	R
	1749 A	1758	K	1766	S
	1750 B	1759	L	1767	T
	1751 C	1760	M	1768	U
George II	1752 D	1761	N	1769	W
1760 George III	1753 E	1762	O	1770	X
	1754 F	1763	P	1771	Y
	1755 G	1764	Q	1772	Z
A	1756 H				

		1781	I	1789	q
	1773 A	1782	I	1790	r
	1774 B	1783	K	1791	f
	1775 C	1784	L	1792	t
George III	1776 D	1785	M	1793	u
	1777 E	1786	N	1794	w
	1778 F	1787	O	1795	x
	1779 G	1788	P	1796	y
A	1780 H				

EXETER

1797	A	1804	H	1811	P	George III
1798	B	1805	I	1812	Q	
1799	C	1806	K	1813	R	
1800	D	1807	L	1814	S	
1801	E	1808	M	1815	T	
1802	F	1809	N	1816	U	
1803	G	1810	O			**A**

1817	a	1824	h	1831	p	George III
1818	b	1825	i	1832	q	1820 George IV
1819	c	1826	k	1833	r	1830 William IV
1820	d	1827	l	1834	s	
1821	e	1828	m	1835	t	
1822	f	1829	n	1836	u	
1823	g	1830	o			**a**

1837	A	1843	G	1850	O	Victoria
1838	B	1844	H	1851	P	
1839	C	1845	I	1852	Q	
1840	D	1846	K	1853	R	
1841	E	1847	L	1854	S	
1842	F	1848	M	1855	T	
		1849	N	1856	U	**A**

51

Victoria [castle]	[castle] [lion] [head]		
	1857 — A	1864 — H	1872 — Q
	1858 — B	1865 — I	1873 — R
	1859 — C	1866 — K	1874 — S
	1860 — D	1867 — L	1875 — T
	1861 — E	1868 — M	1876 — U
	1862 — F	1869 — N	
A	1863 — G	1870 — O	
		1871 — P	

Victoria [castle]	[castle] [lion] [head]		
	1877 — A		
	1878 — B		
	1879 — C		
	1880 — D		
	1881 — E		
A	1882 — F		

GLASGOW

1681	**a**		
1683			
1685			
1689			
1690			

1694	
1696	
1698	
1699	

1700	
1701	
1704	
1705	
1707	**B**
1709	**D**

Charles II

1685
James II

1689
Wm. & My.

1694
William III

1702
Anne

a

1717	
1728	**S**
1734	**S**
1743	**S**
1747	**S**
1756	**S**
1757	

1758	**S**
1763	**E**
1773	**S** **S**
1776	**O**
1783	**S**

1785	**S**
1790	**S**
1795	**S**
1800	**S**
1811	

George I

1727
George II

1760
George III

S

The makers' marks were stamped in duplicate on either side of the town mark up to 1800.

53

GLASGOW

George IV **1830** **William IV** **1837** **Victoria** **A**	1819 **A**	1827 **I**	1837 **S**	
	1820 **B**	1828 **J**	1838 **T**	
	1821 **C**	1829 **K**	1839 **U**	
	1822 **D**	1830 **L**	1840 **V**	
	1823 **E**	1831 **M**	1841 **W**	
	1824 **F**	1832 **N**	1842 **X**	
	1825 **G**	1833 **O**	1843 **Y**	
	1826 **H**	1834 **P**	1844 **Z**	
		1835 **Q**		
		1836 **R**		

Victoria **A**	1845 **A**	1853 **I**	1862 **R**
	1846 **B**	1854 **J**	1863 **S**
	1847 **C**	1855 **K**	1864 **T**
	1848 **D**	1856 **L**	1865 **U**
	1849 **E**	1857 **M**	1866 **V**
	1850 **F**	1858 **N**	1867 **W**
	1851 **G**	1859 **O**	1868 **X**
	1852 **H**	1860 **P**	1869 **Y**
		1861 **Q**	1870 **Z**

54

GLASGOW

🐟🦁👤		1879	Ⓘ	1888	Ⓡ	Victoria
1871	Ⓐ	1880	Ⓙ	1889	Ⓢ	
1872	Ⓑ	1881	Ⓚ	1890	Ⓣ	
1873	Ⓒ	1882	Ⓛ	1891	Ⓤ	
1874	Ⓓ	1883	Ⓜ	1892	Ⓥ	
1875	Ⓔ	1884	Ⓝ	1893	Ⓦ	
1876	Ⓕ	1885	Ⓞ	1894	Ⓧ	Ⓐ
1877	Ⓖ	1886	Ⓟ	1895	Ⓨ	
1878	Ⓗ	1887	Ⓠ	1896	Ⓩ	

🐟🦁🌹		1906	𝒥	🐟🦁🌹		Victoria
1897	𝒜	1907	𝒦	1914	ℛ	1901 Ewd. VII
1898	ℬ	1908	ℒ	1915	𝒮	1910 George V
1899	𝒞	1909	ℳ	1916	𝒯	
1900	𝒟	1910	𝒩	1917	𝒰	
1901	ℰ	1911	𝒪	1918	𝒱	
1902	ℱ			1919	𝒲	
1093	𝒢	1912	𝒫	1920	𝒳	
1904	ℋ			1921	𝒴	
1905	ℐ	1913	𝒬	1922	𝒵	𝒜

GLASGOW

George V 1936 Ewd. VIII 1936 George VI	1923 **a**	1932 **j**	1941 **s**
	1924 **b**	1933 **k**	1942 **t**
	1925 **c**	1934 **l**	1943 **u**
	1926 **d**	1935 **m**	1944 **v**
	1927 **e**	1936 **n**	1945 **w**
	1928 **f**	1937 **o**	1946 **x**
	1929 **g**	1938 **p**	1947 **y**
a	1930 **h**	1939 **q**	1948 **z**
	1931 **i**	1940 **r**	

George VI 1952 Eliz. II	1949 **A**	1956 **M**	
	1950 **B**	1957 **L**	
	1951 **C**	1958 **L**	
	1952 **D**	1959 **M**	
	1953 **E**	1960 **N**	
	1954 **F**	1961 **O**	
21	1955 **G**	1962 **P**	
		1963 **R**	
		In March 1964 the Glasgow Assay Office closed.	

56

NEWCASTLE

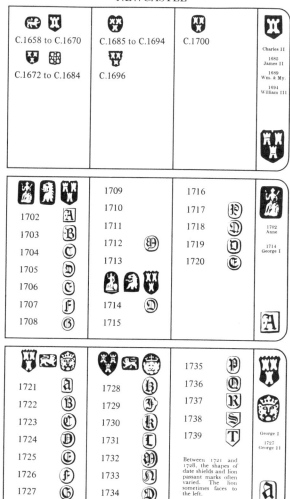

C.1658 to C.1670	C.1685 to C.1694	C.1700	Charles II
C.1672 to C.1684	C.1696		1685 James II
			1689 Wm. & My.
			1694 William III

1702	1709	1716	1702 Anne
1703	1710	1717	1714 George I
1704	1711	1718	
1705	1712	1719	
1706	1713	1720	
1707	1714		
1708	1715		

1721	1728	1735	George I
1722	1729	1736	1727 George II
1723	1730	1737	
1724	1731	1738	
1725	1732	1739	
1726	1733		
1727	1734		

Between 1721 and 1728, the shapes of date shields and lion passant marks often varied. The lion sometimes faces to the left.

George II / A	1740 A	1747 H	1755 Q			
	1741 B	1748 I/J	1756 R			
	1742 C	1749 K	1757 S			
	1743 D	1750 L	1758			
	1744 E	1751 M				
	1745 F	1752 N				
	1746 G	1753 O				
		1754 P				

George II 1760 George III / A	1759 A	1775 I/J	1782 Q
	1760 68 B	1776 K	1783 R
	1769 C	1777 L	1784 S
	1770 D	1778 M	1785 T
	1771 E	1779 N	1786 U
	1772 F	1780 O	1787 W
	1773 G	1781 P	1788 X
	1774 H		1789 Y
			1790 Z

George III / A	1791 A	1799 I/J	1806 Q
	1792 B	1800 K	1807 R
	1793 C	1801 L	1808 S
	1794 D	1802 M	1809 T
	1795 E	1803 N	1810 U
	1796 F	1804 O	1811 W
	1797 G	1805 P	1812 X
	1798 H		1813 Y
			1814 Z

NEWCASTLE

1815 **A**	1823 **I**	1831 **R**
1816 **B**	1824 **K**	1832 **S**
1817 **C**	1825 **L**	1833 **T**
1818 **D**	1826 **M**	1834 **U**
1819 **E**	1827 **N**	1835 **W**
1820 **F**	1828 **O**	1836 **X**
1821 **G**	1829 **P**	1837 **Y**
1822 **H**	1830 **Q**	1838 **Z**

George III
1820 George IV
1830 William IV
1837 Victoria

A

1839 **A**	1846 **H**	1855 **Q**
1840 **B**	1847 **I**	1856 **R**
1841 **C**	1848 **J**	1857 **S**
1842 **D**	1849 **K**	1858 **T**
1843 **E**	1850 **L**	1859 **U**
1844 **F**	1851 **M**	1860 **Y**
1845 **G**	1852 **N**	1861 **W**
	1853 **O**	1862 **X**
	1854 **P**	1863 **Z**

Victoria

A

1864 **a**	1871 **h**	1879 **q**
1865 **b**	1872 **i**	1880 **r**
1866 **c**	1873 **k**	1881 **s**
1867 **d**	1874 **l**	1882 **t**
1868 **e**	1875 **m**	1883 **u**
1869 **f**	1876 **n**	
1870 **g**	1877 **o**	
	1878 **p**	

Victoria

a

NORWICH

Eliz. I / 1603 James I	1565	A	1569	E	1590	
	1566	B			1595	
	1567	C	1570	F	1600	
			1571	G	1610	
			1573	I		
			1574	K		
A	1568	D	1579	P	1620	

James I / 1625 Charles I	With variations		1630	G	1637	O
	1624	A	1631	H	1638	P
	1625	B	1632	I	1639	Q
	1626	C	1633	K	1640	R
	1627	D	1634	L	1641	S
	1628	E	1635	M	1642	T
A	1629	F	1636	N	1643	V

NORWICH

C.1645

C.1650

C.1655

C.1660

C.1665

C.1670

C.1675

C.1680

C.1685

Charles I
1649
Charles II
1685
James II

1688

1689

1691

1696

1697

1701

James II
1689
Wm. & My.
1694
William III

SHEFFIELD

👑 (crown)	🦁	👑	1782	Ⓖ	👑	1791	Ⓟ	👑
George III	1773	Ⓒ		1783	Ⓑ	👑	1792	Ⓤ	👑
	1774	Ⓕ		1784	Ⓖ ⬛ 👑	1793	Ⓞ	👑
	1775	Ⓗ		1785	Ⓟ	👑	1794	Ⓜ	👑
	1776	Ⓡ		🦁 👑 🦁	1795	Ⓠ	👑
Ⓒ	1777	Ⓗ		1786	Ⓚ	👑	1796	Ⓩ	👑
	1778	Ⓢ		1787	Ⓣ	👑	1797	Ⓧ 👑 👑
	1779	Ⓐ		1788	Ⓦ	👑	1798	Ⓥ 👑 👑
	1780	Ⓒ 👑		1789	Ⓝ	👑	July '79 to March '80. The King's Head is duplicated.
👑	1781	Ⓓ 👑		1790	Ⓛ	👑	

👑 (crown)	🦁 👑 🦁	1807	Ⓢ	👑	1816	Ⓣ	👑
George III 1820 George IV	1799	Ⓔ	👑	1808	Ⓟ	👑	1817	Ⓧ	👑
Ⓔ	1800	Ⓝ	👑	1809	Ⓚ	👑	1818	Ⓘ	👑
	1801	Ⓗ	👑	1810	Ⓛ	👑	1819	Ⓥ	👑
	1802	Ⓜ	👑	1811	Ⓒ	👑	1820	Ⓠ	👑
	1803	Ⓕ	👑	1812	Ⓓ	👑	1821	Ⓨ	👑
	1804	Ⓖ	👑	1813	Ⓡ	👑	🦁 🦁 👑
	1805	Ⓑ	👑	1814	Ⓦ	👑	1822	Ⓩ	👑
Ⓢ	1806	Ⓐ	👑	1815	Ⓞ	👑	1823	Ⓤ	👑

			1830	g		1837	r	
1824	a		1831	h		1838	S	
1825	b		1832	k		1839	t	
1826	C		1833	l				
1827	d					1840	u	George IV
			1834	m		1841	V	1830 William IV
1828	e		1835	P		1842	X	1837 Victoria
1829	f		1836	q		1843	Z	a

			1851	H	"	1860	S	
1844	A		1852	I	"	1861	T	Victoria
1845	B		1853	K	"			
1846	C		1854	L		1862	U	
1847	D		1855	M		1863	V	
1848	E		1856	N		1864	W	
1849	F	"	1857	O		1865	X	
1850	G	"	1858	P		1866	Y	
			1859	R		1867	Z	A

63

SHEFFIELD

Victoria	1868 **A**	1876 **J**	1885 **S**
	1869 **B**	1877 **K**	1886 **T**
	1870 **C**	1878 **L**	1887 **U**
	1871 **D**	1879 **M**	1888 **V**
A	1872 **E**	1880 **N**	1889 **W**
	1873 **F**	1881 **O**	1890 **X**
	1874 **G**	1882 **P**	1891 **Y**
	1875 **H**	1883 **Q**	1892 **Z**
		1884 **R**	

Victoria 1901 Ewd. VII 1910 George V	1893 **a**	1901 **i**	1910 **s**
	1894 **b**	1902 **k**	1911 **t**
	1895 **c**	1903 **l**	1912 **u**
	1896 **d**	1904 **m**	1913 **v**
	1897 **e**	1905 **n**	1914 **w**
	1898 **f**	1906 **o**	1915 **x**
	1899 **g**	1907 **p**	1916 **y**
a	1900 **h**	1908 **q**	1917 **z**
		1909 **r**	

SHEFFIELD

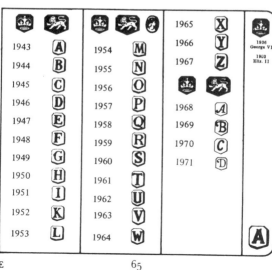

	1926	i
1918	a	
	1927	k
1919	b	
	1928	l
1920	c	
	1929	m
1921	d	
	1930	n
1922	e	
	1931	o
1923	f	
	1932	p
1924	g	
	1933	q
1925	h	
	1934	r
	1935	S

	1936	t
1937	u	
1938	v	
1939	w	
1940	x	
1941	y	
1942	Z	

George V
1936 Ewd. VIII
1936 George VI

a

	1954	M
1943	A	
	1955	N
1944	B	
	1956	O
1945	C	
	1957	P
1946	D	
	1958	Q
1947	E	
	1959	R
1948	F	
	1960	S
1949	G	
	1961	T
1950	H	
	1962	U
1951	I	
	1963	V
1952	K	
	1964	W
1953	L	

	1965	X
	1966	Y
	1967	Z
1968	A	
1969	B	
1970	C	
1971	D	

1936 George VI
1952 Eliz. II

A

	During this period several variations of this town mark may be found.		
Eliz. 1	1562 **D**	1568 **K**	1575 **R**
	1564 **F**	1569 **L**	1576 **S**
		1570 **M**	
	1565 **G**	1572 **O**	1577 **T**
		1573 **P**	
D	1566 **H**	1574 **Q**	1582 **Z**

	During this period several variations of this town mark may be found.		
Eliz. 1 1603 James I	1583 **a**	1592 **k**	1596 **o**
	1584 **b**	1593 **l**	1597 **p**
			1598 **q**
	1587 **e**	1594 **m**	1599 **r**
			1601 **t**
a	1590 **h**	1595 **n**	1604 **x**

		1615 **J**	
	1607 **A**	1616 **K**	1624 **S**
	1608 **B**	1617 **L**	1625 **T**
James 1	1609 **C**	1618 **M**	1626 **U**
1625 Charles 1	1610 **D**	1619 **N**	1627 **W**
	1611 **E**	1620 **O**	
	1612 **F**	1621 **P**	1628 **X**
	1613 **G**	1622 **Q**	1629 **Y**
A	1614 **H**	1623 **R**	1630 **Z**

YORK

🛡		🛡	🛡
1631 *a*	1638 *h*	1650 *t*	Charles 1
1632 *b*	1639 *i*	1651 *u*	1649 Charles 11
1633 *c*	1641 *k*	1652 *v*	
1634 *d*	1642 *l*	1653 *w*	
1635 *e*	1643 *m*	1654 *x*	
1636 *f*	1645 *o*	1655 *y*	
1637 *g*	1649 *s*	1656 *z*	*a*

🛡	1664 *H*	1673 *R*	🛡
	1665 *J*	1674 *S*	
1657 *A*	1666 *K*	1675 *T*	Charles 11
1658 *B*	1667 *L*	1677 *V*	
1659 *C*	1668 *M*	1678 *W*	
1660 *D*	1669 *N*	1679 *X*	
1661 *E*	1670 *O*	1680 *Y*	
1662 *F*	1671 *P*	1681 *Z*	
1663 *G*	1672 *Q*		*A*

🛡	1689 *H*	🛡	🛡
1682 *A*	1690 *J*	1696 *P*	Charles II
1683 *B*	1691 *k*	1697 *Q*	1685 James II
1684 *C*	1692 *L*	1698 *R*	1689 Wm. & My.
1685 *d*	1693 *M*	1699 *S*	1694 William III
1686 *e*	1694 *N*		
1687 *f*	1695 *O*		
1688 *G*			*A*

67

William III	✠ 🦁 🏰		1711	🄦	1782	G
		1700	1713	🄞	1783	H
		1701			1784	J 🦁
		1702	No records for the period 1714 to 1778.		1785	K
1702 Anne 1714 George I		1703	🛡 🦁 👑		1786	L 😐
1727 George II 1760 George III		1705	1778	C		
		1706	1779	D		
𝓐		1708	1780	E		
			1781	F		

George III	🛡 🦁 👑 😐		1795	i	1803	R
		1787	A	1796	k 🦁	1804	S
		1788	B	1797	L	1805	T
		1789	C c	1798	M	1806	U
		1790	d	1799	N	1807	V
		1791	e	1800	O	1808	W
		1792	f	1801	P	1809	X
A		1793	g	1802	Q	1810	Y
		1794	h	🦁 1803 and 1806 sometimes faced right.		1811	Z

George III 1820 George IV 1830 William IV	🛡 🦁 👑 😐		1820	i	1829	s
		1812	a	1821	k	1830	t 😐
		1813	b	1822	l	1831	u
		1814	c	1823	m	1832	v
		1815	d	1824	n	1833	w
		1816	e	1825	o	1834	r
		1817	f	1826	p	1835	y
𝖆		1818	g	1827	q	1836	z
		1819	h	1828	r		

YORK

1837 **A**	1844 **H**	1852 **Q**	
1838 **B**	1845 **I**	1853 **R**	
1839 **C**	1846 **K**	1854 **S**	
1840 **D**	1847 **L**	1855 **T**	
1841 **E**	1848 **M**	1856 **V**	Victoria
1842 **F**	1849 **N**		
1843 **G**	1850 **O**		
	1851 **P**		**A**

William Abdy London 1784	**WA**	Joseph Angel London 1849	**J·A**
Robt Abercromby London 1739	**RA**	Peter Archambo London 1720	**AR**
,, ,, 1740	**Ab**		
Stephen Adams London 1813	**SA**	,, ,, 1722	**PA**
Charles Aldridge & Henry Green London 1775	**H C·A G**	,, ,, 1739	**PA**
Colline Allen Aberdeen 1748	**CA**	Peter Archambo & Peter Meure London 1749	**P·A M**
,, ,, 1748	**CA**	Thomas Bamford London 1719	**Ba**
George Angel London 1850	**GA**		
,, ,, 1861	**GA**	,, ,, 1720	**TB**
,, ,, 1875	**GA**	,, ,, 1739	**TB**
John Angel & George Angel London 1840	**J·A & G·A**	Joseph Barbitt London 1703	**BA**
Joseph Angel & John Angel London 1831	**J·A I·A**	,, ,, 1717	**I·B**
Joseph Angel London 1811	**J·A**	,, ,, 1739	**JB**
		Edward, John & William Barnard London 1846	**E·B J & W**

John Barnard London 1702		Peter, Ann & William Bateman London 1800	
,, ,, 1720			
,, ,, 1720		,, ,, 1800	
James Le Bas Dublin 1810		Peter & Jonathan Bateman London 1790	
,, ,, 1819		,, ,, 1790	
John Backe London 1700		Peter & William Bateman London 1805	
,, ,, 1720		,, ,, 1805	
Harry Beathume Edinburgh 1704		William Bateman London 1815	
Hester Bateman London 1761		Joseph Bird London 1697	
,, ,, 1774		,, ,, 1697	
,, ,, 1776		,, ,, 1724	
,, ,, 1778		William Bond Dublin 1792	
,, ,, 1789			

Maker	Location	Year	Mark
George Boothby	London	1720	
,,	,,	1720	
,,	,,	1739	
James Borthwick	Edinburgh	1681	
Mathew Boulton	Birmingham	1790	
Mathew Boulton & John Fothergill	Birmingham	1773	
Thomas Bolton	Dublin	1701	
,,	,,	1701	
,,	,,	1706	
Thos Bradbury and Sons	Sheffield	1832	
,,	,,	1867	
,,	,,	1878	
,,	,,	1885	
Thos Bradbury and Sons	Sheffield	1889	
,,	,,	1892	
Jonathan Bradley	London	1697	
Robert Breading	Dublin	1800	
,,	,,	1800	
John Bridge	London	1823	
,,	,,	1823	
,,	,,	1823	
Walter Brind	London	1748	
,,	,,	1751	
,,	,,	1751	
,,	,,	1781	
Robert Brook	Glasgow	1673	

Alexander Brown Dublin 1735		John Chartier London 1698	
George Brydon London 1720		,, ,, 1723	
,, ,, 1720		,, ,, 1723	
William Burwash London 1802		Henry Chawner London 1786	
,, ,, 1803		,, ,, 1787	
,, ,, 1813		William Chawner London 1819	
		,, ,, 1820	
William Burwash & Richard Sibley London 1805		,, ,, 1823	
		,, ,, 1833	
John Cafe London 1742		Francis Clarke Birmingham 1836	
,, ,, 1742		Nicholas Clausen London 1709	
William Cafe London 1757		,, ,, 1720	
Robt Calderwood Dublin 1727		Jonah Clifton London 1703	
,, ,, 1760		,, ,, 1720	
William Charnelhouse London 1703		John Clifton London 1708	

MAKERS MARKS

Cocks & Bettridge Birmingham 1806	**C&B**	Edward Cornock London 1723	**EC**
Ebenezer Coker London 1739	**EC**	Augustin Courtauld London 1729	**AC**
,, ,, 1745	**EC**	,, ,, 1739	**AC**
,, ,, 1751	**EC**	Samuel Courtauld London 1746	**SC**
Lawrence Coles London 1697	**CO**	,, ,, 1751	**SC**
John Cooke London 1699		Louisa & Samuel Courtauld London 1777	**LC SC**
Mathew Cooper London 1702		Henry Cowper London 1782	**HC**
		,, ,, 1787	**HC**
,, ,, 1705	**CO**	Paul Crespin London 1720	**CR**
,, ,, 1720	**MC**		
Robert Cooper London 1697	**CO**	,, ,, 1720	**PC**
Thomas Corbet London 1699	**CO**	,, ,, 1739	**PC**
,, ,, 1699	**CO**	,, ,, 1740	**CR**
Edward Cornock London 1707	**CO**	,, ,, 1757	**PC**

74

Joseph Creswick Sheffield 1777	**IC**
Thomas and James Creswick Sheffield 1810	**T&JC**
Thomas, James and Nathaniel Creswick Sheffield 1862	**TJ&NC**
,, ,, 1862	**T·J &N**
William Cripps London 1743	**W·C**
,, ,, 1746	**W·C**
,, ,, 1751	**W·C**
John Crouch London 1808	**J·C**
Francis Crump London 1741	**FC**
,, ,, 1745	**FC**
,, ,, 1750	**FC**
,, ,, 1756	**F·C**
W. & P. Cunningham Edinburgh c.1780	**W& PC**
,, 1790	**W·C PC**

W. & P. Cunningham Edinburgh 1790	**WPC**
Louis Cuny London 1703	**C·V**
Thomas Daniel London 1774	**TD**
,, ,, 1775	**TD**
,, ,, 1783	**T·D**
William Davie Edinburgh 1740	**WD**
,, ,, 1740	**WD**
William Dempster Edinburgh 1742	**W·D**
William Denny London c. 1697	**DE**
William Denny & John Barro 1697	**E DB A**
John Denziloe London 1774	**JD**
Isaac Dighton London 1697	**DI**
John Downes London 1697	**Do**

Nicholas Dumee London 1776		**ND**
John East London 1697		**EA**
John Eckford London 1698		**EC**
,, ,, 1720		**IE**
,, ,, 1725		**EC**
,, ,, 1725		**IE**
,, ,, 1739		**IE**
John Edwards London 1697		**ID**
John Edwards London 1724		**ED**
,, ,, 1724		**I·E**
John Edwards London 1739		**I·E**
,, ,, 1753		**I·E**

Charles Eley London 1825		**CE**
William Eley & George Pierpont London 1777		**WE GP**
William Eley London 1778		**WE**
,, ,, 1785		**WE**
,, ,, 1790		**WE**
,, ,, 1795		**WE**
,, ,, 1795		**WE**
,, ,, 1795		**WE**
,, ,, 1825		**WE**
,, ,, 1826		**WE**
,, ,, 1826		**WE**
William, Charles & Henry Eley London 1824		**WE CE HE**
Elkington, Mason & Co. Sheffield 1859		**EM&Co**

William Elliott London 1813	**WE**	William Fawdery London c. 1697	
John Emes London 1798	**JE**	,, ,, 1720	
,, ,, 1802	**JE**	,, ,, 1720	
Thomas Evans London 1774	**TE**	Edward Feline London 1720	
,, ,, 1779	**TE**	,, ,, 1720	
,, ,, 1782	**TE**	,, ,, 1739	
John Farnell London 1714		William Fleming London c. 1697	
,, ,, 1720		Fenton Brothers Sheffield 1860	
Thomas Farren London 1707		,, ,, 1875	
,, ,, 1739		,, ,, 1883	
John Fawdery London 1697		,, ,, 1888	
,, ,, 1720		,, ,, 1891	
		,, ,, 1896	

Andrew Fogleburg and Stephen Gilbert London 1780		George Fox London 1891	
,, ,, 1780		Charles Thomas and George Fox London 1841	
Thos Folkingham London 1706		James Fraillon London 1710	
,, ,, 1720		,, ,, 1722	
William Fordham London 1706		William Frisby and Paul Storre London 1792	
,, ,, 1720		Daniel Garnier London 1697	
Charles Fox London 1822		Robert Garrard London 1802	
,, ,, 1823		,, ,, 1818	
,, ,, 1823		,, ,, 1822	
,, ,, 1823		,, ,, 1847	
,, ,, 1823		Francis Garthorne London 1697	
,, ,, 1838		George Garthorne London 1697	
George Fox London 1861			
,, ,, 1869			

Dougal Ged Edinburgh 1734		James Gould London 1739	
Pierre Gillois London 1754		,, ,, 1747	
,, ,, 1782		,, ,, 1748	
James Glen Glasgow 1743		William Gould London 1732	
Elizabeth Godfrey London 1741		,, ,, 1734	
John Goode London 1701		,, ,, 1739	
Andrew Goodwin Dublin 1736		,, ,, 1748	
,, ,, 1739		,, ,, 1753	
Hugh Gordon Edinburgh 1744		Robert Gray & Son Glasgow 1819	
		David Green London 1701	
James Gould London 1722		,, ,, 1720	
,, ,, 1722		Henry Greenway London 1775	
,, ,, 1732		William Gwillim London 1740	

William Gwillim & Peter Castle London 1744		Charles Hatfield London 1727	
Hamilton and Inches Edinburgh c. 1880		,, ,, 1727	
John Hamilton Dublin 1717		,, ,, 1739	
,, ,, 1720		Hawksworth Eyre & Co. Sheffield 1833	
Charles Hancock London 1799		,, ,, 1867	
,, ,, 1814		,, ,, 1869	
Charles Frederick Hancock London 1850		,, ,, 1873	
,, ,, 1850		,, ,, 1892	
,, ,, 1870		,, ,, 1894	
,, ,, 1870		Robert Hennell London 1773	
John Hardman & Co. Birmingham 1876		,, ,, 1809	
		,, ,, 1820	
Peter Harrache London 1698		,, ,, 1826	
		,, ,, 1834 (4th generation)	
,, ,, 1698		Robert & David Hennell London 1795 (3rd generation)	

Robert, David & Samuel Hennell London 1802		John Hodson London 1697	
Robert & Samuel Hennell London 1802		William Holmes and Nicholas Dumee London 1773	
Samuel Hennell London 1811		William Holmes London 1776	
Samuel Hennell and John Terry London 1814		Daniel Holy & Co. Sheffield 1776	
Henry Herbert London 1734		,, ,, 1778	
,, ,, 1735		Samuel Hood London 1697	
,, ,, 1739		,, ,, 1720	
,, ,, 1739		Charles Hougham London 1773	
,, ,, 1747		,, ,, 1785	
,, ,, 1747		,, ,, 1786	
Samuel Herbert London 1747		Francis Howden Edinburgh 1781	
Samuel Herbert & Co. London 1750		Thomas Issod London 1697	

John Jacob London 1734		Frederick Kandler London 1758	
,, ,, 1739		Michael Keating Dublin 1779	
,, ,, 1760		,, ,, 1792	
Joseph Jackson Dublin 1799		,, ,, 1854	
Charles Kandler London 1727		William Keats London c. 1697	
,, ,, 1778		,, ,, 1697	
,, ,, 1778		,, ,, 1697	
Charles Kandler & James Murray London 1727		John Keith Banff 1795	
,, ,, 1727		James Ker Edinburgh 1723	
Charles Frederick Kandler London 1735		David King Dublin 1706	
,, ,, 1735		,, ,, 1710	
Frederick Kandler London 1739		George Lambe London 1713	
		Jonathan Lambe London c. 1697	

Paul de Lamerie London 1712		Lea & Clarke Birmingham 1821	
,, ,, 1732		Ledsam, Vale and Wheeler Birmingham 1824	
,, ,, 1739		George Lewis London 1699	
John Lampfert London 1748		Charles Lias London 1837	
,, ,, 1749		John, Henry & Charles Lias London 1830	
Louis Laroche London 1725		John & Henry Lias London 1837	
,, ,, 1739		,, ,, 1839	
Samuel Laundry & Jeffery Griffith London 1731		,, ,, 1843	
Thomas Law Sheffield 1773		,, ,, 1845	
,, ,, 1773		Henry John Lias & Henry John Lias London 1850	
John Lawrence & Co. Birmingham 1826		,, ,, 1853	
Samuel Lea London 1711		,, ,, 1856	
,, ,, 1721		Isaac Liger London 1704	
		,, ,, 1720	

Mathew Linwood Birmingham 1805	ML	William Lukin London 1699	Lu	
John Loyd Dublin 1771	JL	,, ,, 1699	Lu	
Nathaniel Lock London 1698	LO	,, ,, 1725	WL	
,, ,, 1698	LO	Ben. Lumsden Montrose 1788	BL	
,, ,, 1698	LO	Mackay and Chisholm Edinburgh c. 1849	M&C	
Mathew Lofthouse London 1705	QL	Mappin Brothers Sheffield 1856	M&B	
,, ,, 1721	ML	,, ,, 1859	MB	
Mary Lofthouse London 1731	M·L	,, ,, 1867	MB	
Seth Lofthouse London 1697	LO	,, ,, 1867	EM JM	
Edward Lothian Edinburgh 1731	EL	,, ,, 1878	EM JM	
Lothian and Robertson Edinburgh 1746	L&R	,, ,, 1883	C M	
	HG	,, ,, 1885	FC CH	
Robert Lucas London 1726	R·L	,, ,, 1889	F.C C.H	
		,, ,, 1889	.WG JLL	
James Luke Glasgow 1692	IL IL	,, ,, 1893	WG JLL	
		,, ,, 1894	M BROS / Mn Bros	

John Newton Mappin London 1882	**JNM**	Samuel Margas London 1720	**SM**
,, ,, ,, 1883	**JNM**	Thomas Morse London 1720	**MO**
,, ,, ,, 1884	**JNM**	,, ,, 1720	**TM**
,, ,, ,, 1884	**J·N·M**	Marshall & Son Edinburgh c. 1842	**M&S**
,, ,, ,, 1885	**JNM**	Colin McKenzie Edinburgh 1695	**MK**
,, ,, ,, 1886	**JNM**	Lewis Mettayer London 1700	**ME**
John Newton Mappin and George Webb London 1866	**JNM G·W**	,, ,, 1720	**LM**
,, ,, 1880	**J·N·M G.W**	Nathaniel Mills Birmingham 1826	**NM**
Jonathan Madden London 1702	**MA**	Richard Mills London 1755	**R·M**
Mathew Madden London 1697	**MA**	,, ,, 1758	**RM**
Jacob Margas London 1706	**MA**	John Moore Dublin 1729	**IM**
,, . ,, 1720	**IM**	,, ,, 1740	**IM**
Samuel Margas London 1714	**MA**	,, ,, 1745	**M**

Richard Morton Sheffield 1773	**RM**	Mark Paillett London 1698
,, ,, 1773	**RM**	Simon Pantin London 1701
Robert Naughton Inverness 1815	**RN** **RN**	,, ,, 1717
Anthony Nelme London 1697	**Ne**	,, ,, 1720
,, ,, 1722	**N**	Thomas Parr London 1697
Francis Nelme London 1739	**FN**	Thomas Parr Jnr. London 1717
Samuel Neville Dublin 1808	**SN**	,, ,, 1732
Newton & Son Sheffield 1881	**NC**	,, ,, 1739
Henry Nutting & Robt. Hennel London 1808	**HN RH**	,, ,, 1739
Charles Overing London 1697	**Ov**	John Parsons Sheffield 1783
Padley Parkin & Co. Sheffield 1846	**P.P. &Co**	Humphrey Payne London 1701
Padley Stanwell & Co. Sheffield 1857	**PS &C²**	,, ,, 1701
		,, ,, c. 1701
		,, ,, 1739

Edmund Pearce London 1704	**PE**	Peze Pilleau London 1739	
,, ,, 1720	**EP**	John Pittar Dublin 1751	**I·P**
William Peaston London 1745	**WP**	,, ,, 1778	**J·P**
William and Robert Peaston London 1796	**R W*P P**	,, ,, 1813	**J·P**
Samuel Pemberton Birmingham 1784	**SP**	William Pitts London 1789	**WP**
Edward Penman Edinburgh 1706	**EP**	Pierre Platel London 1699	**PL**
James Penman Edinburgh 1705	**P**	Philip Platel London 1737	**PP**
Phipps & Edward Robinson London 1783	**T P E R**	John Pollock London 1734	**I P**
		Thomas Powell London 1756	**TP**
		,, ,, 1758	**TP**
Mathew Pickering London 1703	**PI**	Joseph Preedy London 1777	**I*P**
Peze Pilleau London 1720	**P·P**	,, ,, 1800	**IP**
		John Pringle Perth 1827	**IP**
,, ,, 1720	**PI**	,, ,, 1827 **I·P**	**I·P**

87

Benjamin Pyne London c. 1710		Patrick Robertson Edinburgh 1751	
,, ,, c. 1720		John (later Lord) Rollo Edinburgh 1731	
Phillip Rainaud London 1707		Phillip Rollos London 1697	
,, ,, 1720		,, ,, 1697	
John Rand London 1703		,, ,, 1705	
Samuel Roberts Sheffield 1773		,, ,, 1720	
Samuel Roberts Jnr. & George Cadman Sheffield 1786		Philip Rundell London 1819	
,, ,, 1786		,, ,, 1819	
Roberts & Belk Sheffield 1864		,, ,, 1822	
,, ,, 1864		Abraham Russell London 1702	
,, ,, 1892		John le Sage London 1722	
,, ,, 1869		,, ,, 1739	
,, ,, 1879		,, ,, 1739	

A. B. Savory London	1826		Daniel Shaw London	1748
,, ,,	1826		William Shaw London	1727
,, ,,	1826		,, ,,	1728
,, ,,	1826		,, ,,	1739
,, ,,	1826		,, ,,	1745
,, ,,	1826		,, ,,	1748
,, ,,	1836		William Shaw & William Priest London	1749
John Schuppe London	1753		,, ,,	1750
John Scofield London	1778		W. & G. Sissons Sheffield	1858
,, ,,	1787		Gabriel Sleath London	1706
Digby Scott and Benjamin Smith London	1802		,, ,,	1706
,, ,,	1803		,, ,,	1720
William Scott Banff	1680		,, ,,	1739
James Seabrook London	1714		Gabriel Sleath & Francis Crump London	1753
,, ,,	1720			

Benjamin Smith London 1807	**BS**	
Daniel Smith & Robert Sharp London 1780	**DS RS**	
,, ,, 1780	**DS RS**	
,, ,, 1780	**R D·S S**	
Edward Smith Birmingham 1833	**ES**	
James Smith London 1718	**S·M**	
,, ,, 1720	**I·S**	
,, ,, 1744	**I·J**	
Stephen Smith London 1865	**S.S**	
,, ,, 1878	**S·S·**	
,, ,, 1880	**SS**	
Paul Storr London 1799	**P·S**	

Paul Storr London 1807	**PS**	
,, ,, 1808	**PS**	
,, ,, 1817	**PS**	
,, ,, 1834	**PS**	
John Sutton London 1697	**SV**	
Thomas Sutton London 1711	**SU**	
John Swift London 1739	**I·S**	
,, ,, 1739	**I·S**	
,, ,, 1757	**I·S**	
James Sympsone Edinburgh 1687	**S**	
,, ,, 1687	**I·S**	
Richard Syng London 1697	**Sy**	
,, ,, 1697	**Sy**	

Benjamin Tait Dublin 1791	**BT**
James Tait Edinburgh 1704	
Ann Tanqueray London 1713	**AT**
David Tanqueray London 1713	**TA**
,, ,, 1720	**DT**
Joseph Taylor Birmingham 1812	**IT**
Samuel Taylor London 1744	**ST**
Taylor & Perry Birmingham 1834	**T&P**
Thomas Tearle London 1739	**TT**
Edward Thomason Birmingham 1817	**ET**
,, ,, 1817	**ET**
William Townsend Dublin 1734	**T.W**
,, ,, 1734	**WT**
,, ,, 1753	**W.T**
John Tuite London 1739	**IT**
William Tuite London 1756	**WT**
Joseph Turner Birmingham 1838	**I·T**
George Unite Birmingham c. 1838	**GU**
Archibald Ure Edinburgh 1717	**AU**
Ayme Videau London 1739	**AV**
Edward Vincent London 1739	**E.V.**
Edward Wakelin London 1747	**EW**
John Wakelin & William Taylor London 1776	**I.W W.T**
,, ,, 1777	**I.W W.T**
Joseph Walker Dublin 1701	**JW**
Samuel Walker Dublin 1738	**SW**

MAKERS MARKS

Thomas Walker Dublin 1723	
Walker Knowles & Co. Sheffield 1836	WK &Co
Joseph Ward London 1697	
Samuel Wastell London 1701	W.A
,, ,, 1701	W·A
Mathew West Dublin 1776	MW
Gervais Wheeler Birmingham 1835	GW
Thomas Whipham London 1737	T.W
,, ,, 1739	TW
Thomas Whipham & Charles Wright London 1757	
Thos. Whipham and Wilm. Williams London 1740	
Fuller White London 1744	FW

Fuller White London 1750	F·W
,, ,, 1758	FW
John White London 1719	Wh
,, ,, 1724	IW
,, ,, 1730	IW
George Wicke London 1721	W·I
,, ,, 1721	GW
,, ,, 1735	GW
Starling Wilford London 1717	WI
,, ,, 1720	SW
,, ,, 1729	SW
David Willaume London 1718	WI
,, ,, 1718	WI
,, ,, 1728	WI
,, ,, 1728	DW

MAKERS MARKS

David Willaume London 1734		Edward Wood London 1740	
Richard Williams Dublin 1761		Samuel Wood London 1733	
,, ,, 1775		,, ,, 1737	
Wilm. Williamson Dublin 1773		,, ,, 1739	
,, ,, 1747		,, ,, 1754	
Joseph Willmore Birmingham 1806		William Woodard London 1741	
Thomas Willmore Birmingham 1789		John Wren London 1777	
,, ,, 1796		Charles Wright London 1775	
John Winter & Co. Sheffield 1836		,, ,, 1780	
John Wirgman London 1751		James Young London 1775	
Edward Wood London 1722		John Young & Co. Sheffield 1779	
,, ,, 1722		,, ,, 1779	
,, ,, 1735			